BITCOIN
FOR BEGINNERS

How to Buy Bitcoins

Sell Bitcoins and Invest in Bitcoins

J.T. Jackman

Disclaimer

Table of Contents

Chapter One

Meet the Bitcoin

If you were to research Bitcoins you would find a lot of things said about them during their very short lifespan.

For example, in an article in the *New York Times* of November 26, 2013, one expert called them everything from "zany" and "weird" to "speculative" and the "currency of the future".

How can something that doesn't physically exist, being essentially a string of numbers hosted in an online ledger, fall under so many descriptions and terms?

It is because Bitcoins are still evolving - even as we speak. They are less than five years in age and are popular for many different reasons. They don't belong to any sort of banking institution. They are part of a decentralized network of computers, and they are the end result of a lot of complex mathematical calculations and equations.

They are also created with a firm cap in sight (21 million is the total number that can ever be created), and are traded on a peer to peer system that rewards computer hosts with newly created Bitcoins as well.

They bypass all of the fees and limitations of credit card companies and standard payment processors. They are both very public and yet entirely private, and are authenticated in a way that guards against fraud to the greatest extent possible.

As said in that *New York Times* article, Bitcoin is "*...digital cash, offering the same relative anonymity and freedom as a paper sack of bills.*"

Now, you might argue that such a description is just one person's opinion, and that it is only time that will tell if Bitcoins are here to stay. And while it is true that we each have an opinion, we also have the facts.

For instance, the author of this "op-ed" piece cited above was also the same journalist who first broke the news of Bitcoins back in 2011, and someone who has been actively watching the growth of this unique currency.

More importantly, this journalist was the first to see and to describe just how Bitcoins were being used in a large number of ways, and usually for the benefits that come with anonymity. That anonymity is still one of the "selling points" for those new to Bitcoins, but there is a lot more to the story.

What Kind of Coins?

Of course, you may be like millions of would-be buyers and investors and ask "Just what the heck is a Bitcoin anyway?" And that is the focus of this book.

We are going to look at Bitcoins in terms of:

- *What they are;*

- *How to obtain them;*

- *How to store and use them;*

- *Whether they are a good investment; and*

- *Where they are headed.*

Though you might go online and find a handful of sites offering to explain Bitcoins, you will end up like millions of others - scratching your head and saying "Huh?" This is because there are a lot of different facts or truths about them, including:

You will read that "miners" create them.

You will read that they are not actually coins, but lines of code and "inputs".

You will hear about anonymous cryptographers and groups of programmers seeking solutions to complex mathematical problems.

You will quickly see that the technicalities of Bitcoins will boggle the average reader's mind.

So, to keep it as simple as possible:

- Bitcoins are viewed as a form of "digital currency". This means that they are not an actual, physical currency such as a dollar or a bar of gold.

- They are not in the hands of a bank either. Instead, Bitcoins are stored in computers spread all across the Internet.

- They belong to a network of buyers and investors and they are used as a payment system as much as currency.

- They are anonymous and yet the system and all of the transactions are public. (Don't worry   we'll explain!)

- They are, as Wired suggested, "a re-imagining of
  international finance, something that breaks down
  barriers between countries and frees currency from
  the control of federal governments"

However, they are "virtual" and that is something that a lot of
consumers just cannot get their heads around. Of course, it is
very useful if you take the time to understand what is known
as a "fiat" economy. So let's turn our gaze toward that for a
brief moment.

The Fiat Economic Model

The technicalities of Bitcoins are many. We are going to
explain most of them to you throughout this guide, but you
have to begin any education about them by understanding
just how they are a form of currency.

After all, there is no bank and no federal government backing
Bitcoin currency. Instead, they are digital files that are listed

in ledger form on the entire network. The files and numbers don't actually represent anything in the "real" or physical world. They have value because people are now willing to exchange real goods and services to create a higher or lower number on their account, and because they believe that the others using this system are going to do the same. The numbers associated with Bitcoins only have value because those using them believe that they do - just as in all fiat currencies and systems.

After all, that $20 in your wallet only has that much purchasing power because you and the store you use it in both agree that it does. That is fiat at work. The paper has extrinsic value - outside value assigned by another - rather than being like gold or platinum which has value on its own, or intrinsic value.

This means that your Bitcoins have no intrinsic value. They have no value in and of themselves. Instead, they derive their value because (as is the case with the American dollar bill) they are something that people want.

Note: This is the classic supply versus demand model as well as the fiat system.

Supply Versus Demand Drives Value and Stabilizes Economy

Bitcoins are something that *a lot* of people want, in fact, and because they are in limited supply they continue to increase in value.

In 2011, a Bitcoin cost around $9. As of the writing of that op-ed above, a Bitcoin was priced between $790 and $880 (depending on your chosen source), and around the Thanksgiving holiday of 2013, the *New York Times* reported that they were spiking towards $1,000. That tells us that Bitcoins are more than just "zany" and are something to give plenty of attention to.

Additionally, the dominance of the Internet and mobile devices also means that anything that can be used effectively with them is likely to be a success. After all, how often do most people even carry cash these days? If, instead of handing over debit or credit card numbers and leaving yourself vulnerable to hackers, you could use Bitcoins to make an untraceable and (so far) unhackable transaction, wouldn't you?

The fiat aspect of Bitcoins is something that a lot of investors worry about because it means you can rely on currency that is still developing and fluctuating a bit wildly. However, most financial experts are saying that they see Bitcoin as the first virtual currency likely to succeed.

There have been other attempts, but none were yet able to garner the same sort of foothold as Bitcoin. The point, however, is that just as so much is going virtual, online, and out of the tangible or "brick and mortar" world, so too is currency.

Virtual is Here to Stay

Unfortunately, as you start to learn more about Bitcoins, it is likely that you will hear from the many famous "naysayers" who worry that Bitcoins are a fad or a trend that is likely to "bust" or to fail to grow into a full blown currency.

However, the signs all indicate that Bitcoins are a true success story.

In addition to their soaring prices, and the enormous number of "miners" (something we'll look at shortly), more and more vendors and businesses are accepting payments in Bitcoins.

For instance, billionaire tycoon Richard Branson's Virgin Airlines now accepts Bitcoin payments for trips to outer space offered by his firm. And if this savvy business expert is willing to take them, it is a clear indicator of their validity as a form of workable currency.

An online article had a lot to say about all forms of virtual currency (not just Bitcoins, though it repeatedly cites them as the only proven success).

However, one of the most substantial points was that we have to all get "used to the idea of virtual currency…the fact that there are so many types of virtual currency shows that this is a concept that is not going away." (Zeiler)

Financial Independence

The article also pointed out that even a virtual and fiat currency so new to the world can serve an extremely important function - it can enable money transfers to any part of the world, and can do so without the standard interferences of banks and payment firms. It effectively removes the often harmful and costly "middlemen" and instead stands alone.

A decentralized currency of this kind puts the funds of the individual entirely outside of the control (and possible harm) of a government or a central banking system. This releases the individual from the risks in the standard markets while giving consumers a way of buying and investing that is entirely anonymous. It is why political parties like the Libertarians are so excited about them - complete economic freedom.

So, this tells us that there is a tremendous amount to know about Bitcoins, and the sooner we roll up our sleeves and get into the information, the faster you can make your decisions about how to add them to a portfolio or even use them as your preferred currency.

Chapter Two

History of Bitcoins

Standard wisdom tells us that the best way to begin is at the beginning. This means we need to look at the history of Bitcoins to really get a firm grasp on what they are and how they are important to anyone in the modern economy.

Not Long Ago

Though technology has been expanding like the proverbial wild fire over the past few decades, the speed at which Bitcoins have been taken up might make even the most modern person's head spin.

In 2009 a programmer (or a group of them - no one knows and it is now believed that no one will ever know *that* part of the story) under the name of Satoshi Nakamoto released a software system for Bitcoins in Japan. From there it has taken off like wildfire. However, a lot feel that who or whatever Satoshi Nakamoto is, it is based in Japan.

Not only did the software originate there, but one of the largest exchanges is there too. This leads many to believe that it is a Japanese individual or group that has created Bitcoin, but to date there is not yet any verification of the origins of Bitcoin a creator(s).

Very little is known about this person or persons, except that only a year earlier a white paper had been released that outlined the feasibility for the use of digital currency.

From the release of that white paper in 2008, the timeline looks like this:

- 2009 - Nakamoto releases a massive assortment of complex algorithms to create Bitcoins as virtual currency. The initial program allows anyone to solve math problems and receive Bitcoins. This has come to be known as "mining". At this time it also becomes possible to buy Bitcoins from formal exchanges.

NOTE: At this point in the timeline it is indicated that there will always be a finite number of Bitcoins possible - 21 million - and this figure still holds true.

- 2010 - An online order for a pizza was paid for in Bitcoins. This is only three months after the marketplace was firmly established. It cost a whopping 10k in Bitcoins!

- 2011 - BitPay, the first official payment processor allowing merchants to accept Bitcoins appears. It is a true exchange in that it allows the users and senders to remain anonymous by transferring their Bitcoins in digital "wallets" that can be created on mobile devices or computers. The program in BitPay actually tracks every Bitcoin to eliminate counterfeiters from corrupting the system.

- Also in 2011, Media attention from the now famous Silk Road Drug scandal attracts global attention to Bitcoins. Though barely at $10 each at the opening of the year, by the middle of 2011 the coins are priced at $32.

- Mid-2012 is when the Bitcoin Foundation is created. It is a trade group that puts an emphasis on creating Bitcoin standards. The only goal of the Foundation is to ensure that Bitcoins become a trusted currency. They do this by collectively investing in a stronger infrastructure that gives the Bitcoin network/community even more stability.

At this same time many large and small clubs and start-ups appear with the use, expansion, or solutions for Bitcoin use as a collective goal. Coinbase in California is one example, but so too is the Paly

Entrepreneurs Club (a group of high school students who built a Bitcoin trading network).

- In 2013, the Bitcoin gets a tremendous boost when the Libertarian Party begins accepting political donations through BitPay.

- Even more encouraging to the growth of Bitcoins is the fact that in March of this year the nation of Cyprus plummets into economic turmoil and the country's financial experts suggest that citizens transfer their personal holdings into Bitcoins. This causes the price of a Bitcoin to jump to $90.

- Early in 2013 the validity of Bitcoins is reinforced when the Treasury Department's Financial Crimes Enforcement Network in the United States gives preliminary guidelines to money transfer firms such as Western Union about virtual currency.

- It is also in early 2013 that the collective value of all Bitcoins in existence exceeded one billion dollars. The famous Winklevoss twins have, by this point in the Bitcoin timeline already amassed what is thought to be one of the largest portfolios of them. Silicon Valley is giving Bitcoin a tremendous amount of attention.

- In April and May of 2013 one of the biggest Bitcoin exchanges has its accounts frozen in the U.S. by the Department of Homeland Security.

- In September of 2013, SecondMarket begins fundraising for its Bitcoin Investment Trust.

- In early November of 2013 the Bitcoin price breaks $800 and keeps climbing.

So, in a little less than five years' time the Bitcoin went from theory, to concept, to global success story.

How they Work

Now that you know how they began with the Nakamoto program, it becomes a bit easier to see how you might begin to buy and invest in Bitcoins. However, let's go over the very basic information of how they work just to be sure:

1. The Network - It all begins with the Bitcoin network designed using that initial and somewhat unique programming. The network is built with the many computers spread around the world that do all of the "mining".

    They are decentralized and their work is to verify transactions, maintain the "ledger" (also called the blockchain) relating to all Bitcoin transactions. This ledger is updated automatically whenever transactions occur.

    Today, you can still purchase mining hardware and seek to earn Bitcoins through mining efforts, but the competition has become quite fierce, and it requires immense computing power to win the race of mining.

2. The miners actually drive the system and anyone can become a host. However, it does demand the kind of processing power and software necessary.

Essentially, the more miners the more power to the network. This is why miners pursue 25 new Bitcoins as a reward given to those who operate the hardware. As an article in the Wall Street Journal explained:

   a. Miners attempt to guess solutions to increasingly difficult math problems, while recording Bitcoin transfers in the process, for which they're awarded Bitcoins.

   b. As more miners enter the network, competition to find solutions also increases, and as more Bitcoins are created, the potential payoff falls.

c. The system is designed so that the total number of Bitcoins won't exceed 21 million. (Light)

So, you can see that mining may still be a viable way to get a steady supply of Bitcoins, but it takes heavy duty gear and processing power. This is why "pools" are becoming a much more common method of earning Bitcoins. (We consider this a bit later in the book)

3. Computers in the network are called "nodes" and they each broadcast and receive data relating to every transaction. This is what distinguished Bitcoin from standard banks or financial exchanges - there is nothing private.

Unlike a bank, the Bitcoin network allows everyone to see everyone else's transactions. The ledger is maintained openly by a group and this actually ensures security rather than jeopardizing it.

The thing to remember is that you will never see a line item in the ledger such as "Bob Jones - 10 Bitcoins - Beer and Wine Store". Instead, it is just a long and complex series of numbers that, if you have the right software, identifies the keys and signatures.

Nodes (computers on the network) receive broadcasts of exchanges and update their copy of the ledger. They know that this is authentic because the fundamental rules of the Bitcoin software require "Digital Signatures" (a type of password) to use funds. This password authenticates any message going through the network and essentially eliminates any risks of forgery or theft.

However, the Digital Signature has to be attached to every transaction and it is made of two very different parts - a "Private Key" and a "Public Key". The Private Key is what creates the signature while the Public Key is what others on the network can use to check it.

Think of it this way:

- A private key is the true password and only you know it.

- The signature is the intermediary that demonstrates that you have the password without also making you reveal it.

- Public keys are a sort of "send to" command in the address in Bitcoin software

- When you send someone money it is directed to THEIR public key. (Driscoll)

In order to spend Bitcoins you have to prove you own that Public Key, and this is why that Digital Signature is necessary.

All of the nodes in the network can then take what is needed from the Signature (the Public Key) to document the transaction.

Of course, just as with any password - you can lose it, forget it, or somehow delete the information from the computer. However, unlike other systems or sites, should your password be lost or stolen, the Bitcoins associated with them are also lost or stolen forever.

The good news is that all of this is relatively simple if you have the open source software and a computer capable of handling the processing.

4. Naturally, you can take a shortcut around this and never work as a miner at all. Nor do you need to keep track of everything in this way. There are several alternatives for the ways that Bitcoins work, and you can rely on far simpler methods of getting and using Bitcoins and signatures, and they are:

   a. Setting up a "hot" Bitcoin wallet - this is using software on a computer that links to the Bitcoin network and allows you to securely and easily make transactions with Bitcoins you purchase using actual currency;

   b. Setup a "mobile" Bitcoin wallet - this puts software on a mobile device that allows you to safely use Bitcoin in the "real world". Usually it is done by scanning a QR code displayed in a retail shop in order to complete a sale or transaction;

c. Create an online wallet - you can use websites that allow you to send, receive, and safely store your Bitcoins without actually installing any software on your computer;

d. Shop at stores that use Bitcoin systems - there are stores online that are already connected to the Bitcoin network;

e. Using a Bitcoin exchange - there are many online exchanges where you are able to just "trade" currency for Bitcoins. These are not as anonymous as other forms because they require connections to real world banks. However, they allow you to move Bitcoins directly into a bank account or the reverse;

f. Create a "cold" wallet - this is simply using a computer that remains "offline" to store your

Bitcoin data. It is the only way to eliminate any threat of hacking;

g. Real world Bitcoin exchanges - many people opt to meet in person to exchange real world currencies for Bitcoins. They will meet in a public place and then conduct an exchange of money when the other person transmits Bitcoins across the network; and

h. Physical Bitcoin exchanges - many people worry about hackers and opt to store all of their Bitcoin keys in the real world. They do this by writing them down, engraving them on an item, or actually acquiring coins with the cryptographic keys engraved on them.

5. Also note that you don't have to panic about the idea of a Bitcoin being required to purchase things. After all, why use something valued at $1000 for a cup of

coffee? Bitcoins, luckily, are highly divisible and you don't have to use a full Bitcoin at any time.

A "satoshi" is one millionth of a Bitcoin and you are allowed to send as little as 5430 satoshis in a transaction over the network. (That would mean that if a Bitcoin is worth $1000, you can spend as little as $5.34 in a transaction)

6. Investments are also done through direct purchases of Bitcoins, and most occur online through web based firms. Currently, the most common are Mt. Gox, Coinbase, and Bitstamp among many others.

Now, you can just buy your Bitcoins and use them to conduct the most private business and exchanges possible. You can also buy them as a sort of protest against all of the monetary systems. Additionally, you might elect to use them as a form of investment.

For example, earlier in this book we indicated that you could have purchased a Bitcoin for around $9 only a year ago, and as of November 25, 2013 you could have sold that same coin for up to $880.

This shows that it may make a tremendous amount of sense to monitor the prices of Bitcoins. Over their short lifetime they have experienced a few roller coaster like changes in value, but as one expert pointed out, they tend to always come out in a better position than before a decline.

Now you know the basics of how Bitcoins work. You can certainly invest in mining gear, or you can convert a portion of your portfolio into Bitcoin. You can also get a wallet and use several ways to turn currency into Bitcoin and begin using your wallet to make payments wherever possible.

You might even find an ATM that converts Bitcoin to currency! In Vancouver, Canada you can use a special kiosk that features hand and barcode scanners that move funds to or from the virtual wallet - with a limit of up to $1,000 in transfers per day.

All of this might leave you wondering "How do I get started?" Before we head into building the online wallet and converting assets into Bitcoins, let's really focus on mining as this is a very important facet of the Bitcoin world. Whether you want to be a miner or not, you really should understand how this part of the process works since it is the foundation of the currency and will have an eventual impact on the supply and the value of Bitcoins.

Some Words on Mining

Before we move away from a discussion about how Bitcoins work, let's direct attention to mining a bit longer.

A lot of "newbies" to the world of Bitcoins will allow themselves to believe that mining is a very easy thing if you have a computer and software. However, it is not a simple thing to do and it grows increasingly more challenging each day and with each new headline about the increasing values of Bitcoins.

How to Mine

Let's look at a summary of steps required:

1. Every Bitcoin transaction is collected by the network (remember that Bitcoin is an actual network hosted by many decentralized computers) and organized into "blocks". The blocks are a snapshot of transactions that occurred in a very fixed window of time.

2. Miners are going to confirm transactions and write them in that ledger mentioned much earlier in this book. So, the ledger is just a very long list of the different blocks. This is why the other name for the ledger is the block chain.

3. The purpose of the ledger is validation as it can allow you to actually look at every transaction made between two Bitcoin addresses at any location on the network.

4. Every single transaction is written to the block chain, and this means that the list is always growing and that an updated copy of this block is shared across the network at regular, fixed, intervals.

5. Now, you might say that it would be fairly simple to somehow manipulate this data and commit fraud, but it is far more complicated. How? The miners on the network actually process data in a way that makes it almost impervious to tampering.

6. It begins when miners receive a block and put it through an algorithm that converts that block into another form. This form is much smaller and shorter

and uses a series of numbers and letters that are called a "hash".

7. Each hash is stored with its block at the end of that block chain.

8. Though it is a simple thing to create that hash from an assortment of data, it is nearly impossible to "read" that data by reviewing the hash. Why? Every hash is unique. If you attempt to alter it by just one number or character in the Bitcoin block, it changes the hash entirely.

9. Even this might be a system open to tampering but miners use more than just the transactions documented in a block to create each hash. Among them are some pieces of data that were from the hash of the previous block in the chain.

10. Simply put: Every hash is the result of the hash of the block before it, and that means that confirmation can only come from a fully legitimate hash. Attempting to "fake" a transaction within a block that has already been put into the chain will change that block's hash. It will also create a chain reaction should the hash be checked because every previous hash would also read as fake too.

11. This brings us to the way that a miner can earn Bitcoins. When they are able to "seal" a block using the software designed to validate them, they create a hash. When they do that, they get a reward of 25 Bitcoins. This creates an update on the network, and every node is alerted to this "solution".

12. Recall that any explanations of Bitcoins always begin with a sentence such as "miners compete to solve complex mathematical equations in order to get rewarded with Bitcoins". Well, that is the equation

they seek to solve - they want to seal the block by finding the hash.

13. However, although it might seem that almost any modern computer would be able to create a new hash from a fixed assortment of data (a block); Bitcoin software does not make it that easy.

14. The protocol in the software has something known as a "proof of work" required as well. This means that a hash has to be formatted in a specific way. It has to have a set number of zeroes at the beginning, and there is absolutely no way of knowing what any hash is going to look like before it is produced. When any new data is added the hash is going to be different too.

15. Confused? Bitcoin protocols want you to be. Otherwise, there would already be millions of Bitcoins awarded to miners. Even at this point there

is more demanded from the miner. Even though the miner cannot alter any transaction data in a block it must do so to create a new and different hash. They can succeed in this through the use of a "nonce". This is integrated with the data to generate the new hash and if this doesn't work, the nonce is altered and the data hashed again. Clearly, it can take a lot to integrate a nonce that actually works with the data, and miners are all racing to get to this solution. When they do, they get their Bitcoins.

To really summarize the mining process, just accept that it actually doesn't "compute" anything special. It is looking for a number, which in combination with the "payload", results in a "hash" with very specific properties. The payload is essentially data that relates to activity in the official Bitcoin network and is integrated with the appropriate nonce. This is what is known as the "hash", and is what is rewarded with Bitcoin.

Yes, very complex and getting more so every single day. In fact, one report indicates that all of the computers competing for 25 Bitcoins must each do around 5 quintillion mathematical calculations per second in order to get the prize. This translates to roughly 150 times the number of operations that the most powerful super computers in the world handle. (Wired)

All of this may make you wonder how anyone might view mining as simple. However, there are many ways to obtain hardware that can allow you to get started right away.

Hardware, Energy, and Markets are Part of Mining

As most experts warn, there are three categories of Bitcoin mining gear and each is going to be more powerful but more expensive than the last.

This is why you must calculate the potential for profitability in any mining venture. You do so by finding:

- Equipment costs

- Hash rate

- Energy consumption

- Current Bitcoin prices (this is to gauge what the rate of return is on the investment)

Let's explore these issues briefly:

- Equipment costs - There are three kinds of hardware available for Bitcoin mining and they are:

    o CPUs or GPUs - The least costly and the least powerful, they tend to need further hardware added to ensure that they can do all of that processing. As you might have guessed, CPUs

44

are the standard processors on your laptop or desktop system, and clearly, these will never have the computing power of a super computer or greater.

Because of this, anyone hoping to go the CPU route is going to have to improve the hash rate through the installation of additional graphics hardware or cards. This is where "GPUs" enter the equation. They are graphical processing units that can do the brute force and so-called heavy lifting so necessary to calculate the hashing calculations required to seal or solve blocks.

Two of the most frequently chosen makers are Nvidia and ATI. The cards are not inexpensive and can run in the hundreds of dollars. However, they are essential if you are going to use the CPU for hashing.

NOTE: A plus where this approach is concerned is the simple fact that GPUs work with any other "cryptocurrencies" or virtual currencies. You can put them to use with algorithms for other currencies similar to Bitcoin in the future, or you can switch between networks to maximize returns. However, to compete with the two other hardware types you will need to have a motherboard capable of accepting many boards.

o FPGAs - Field Programmable Gate Array, this works with only one type of virtual currency processing and will have to be Bitcoin specific. It is, however, a completely customizable and high volume processing approach to mining that is considered superior to CPU/GPU.

- ○ ASICs - Application Specific Integrated
  Circuits are the top of the line and are meant
  to work at low energy consumption, high
  speed, and specifically in the Bitcoin realm.
  This hardware is meant for one thing - Bitcoin
  mining. It can often do so at the super
  computer speed, and can already hit speeds of
  500 GH/sec. You can buy "turnkey units"
  from such vendors as Avalon, Butterfly Labs,
  CoinTerra, and KnCMiner.

- Hash rate - As you might guess, this is just the
  number of calculations the hardware is capable of
  performing every second. It is going to be seeking to
  solve a very complex problem and so the rates of
  measurement are substantial. They read as
  megahashes, gigahashes, and terahashes per second
  (MH/sec, GH/sec, and TH/sec). Obviously, the
  faster the processing power the more likely you are to

get the solution ahead of everyone else. Of course, the flipside is that the faster the hash rate, the more costly the device. Some good sources of information around the best hardware and top hash rates are the Bitcoin wiki page's Mining hardware comparison https://en.bitcoin.it/wiki/Mining_hardware_compari son and the Genesis Block http://mining.thegenesisblock.com/ statistics page.

- Energy consumption - As you might also have guessed here, the computing done during mining is pretty intense and this can gobble up a lot of energy. This impacts the bottom line of your mining efforts and has to be taken into consideration. After all, there are many stories of fellow miners who end up spending most or all of their money on electricity. As you begin looking at hardware and hash rates, also keep in mind that you should utilize any data or formulations run on energy consumption or usage.

For instance, you might see hardware that features an Mhash/J calculation. This is a ratio depicting how many millions of hashes are run per joule of energy. It is essentially an energy efficiency ratio that describes how many watts are used. If one joule is the same as one watt per second, it would mean that the "J" in the equation means 1 watt.

- Profitability - You must look at the current pricing on Bitcoins as well as a few other parameters to determine if your hardware and investment is profitable. For example, as the ASIC devices drop in price, news of Bitcoin values spreads, and more people start mining, the difficulty of using the network increases. This reflects a negative direction in the profitability because it becomes more and more difficult to solve transaction blocks before anyone else. Use the cost of the equipment, hash rate, power consumption, network difficulty, and Bitcoin prices to calculate your rate of return.

Once you have discovered your gear and made the investment, it is time to download the software too. When using GPUs and FPGAs, you need a host computer running two things: the standard Bitcoin client, and the mining software.

You may need the mining software for an ASIC miner, though the latest releases of the hardware actually arrive pre-configured.

The Bitcoin client is what gets you on the network and allows you to enjoy peer to peer activities as conduct mining operations. You will be interacting with Bitcoin clients, moving transactions forward, and participating in the maintenance of the block chain. This is such a high volume of information that it takes a lot of time for the initial download of the complete Bitcoin block chain.

After this is done, however, the Bitcoin client then relays any and all messages and information from your mining gear to the network. This includes news from the creator of the programming to updates about recent Bitcoin rewards.

Then there is Bitcoin mining software. This is specialty software that controls your hardware and essentially determines the outcome of your investment. It is what feeds the transaction blocks to the system and it will operate on standard OS, Windows, and other accepted operating systems.

Getting in the Pools

The last thing to know about mining is that you can join "pools" that are like a collective of computers. Essentially, you add your computing power to the rest of the group's and you all work together to generate a block and hash. The rewards are then shared throughout the group. However, it is not just a network of connected systems. Each "client" or miner is going to "share" their work with others. Rewards can be based on recent shares, on a per share basis, rolled in from other projects, and more. There are also fees associated with pools, and this is something that a miner has to add to their calculations around profitability.

Naturally, you want to work with pools utilizing approaches that cut down on or eliminate cheating to ensure you're not doing a lot of work and rewarding others for it. There are a few approaches used in mining, and several well established pools.

For instance, the BTC Guild currently has around 30% of the finds with more than 15k blocks found. Their "luck" rate is 96.55% (per BitcoinChain) and clearly they are a successful "guild".

However, before we look at the profitability of pools, let's look at the approaches used to help you recognize any you might want to join.

The Approaches Used in Pools

It is agreed that multiple generating clients will help to generate a block much faster than individual client cranking out calculations. However, pooling resources does reduce the size of the reward and open the door to cheating.

These both have to be taken into consideration. For one thing, as the value of Bitcoins increase pooling is more rewarding.

After all, it doesn't sound silly for a group to share a $25k prize, while it does seem odd for a large number to seek to split a far less substantial one. This is why pools don't always work on a flat rate fee of Bitcoins when blocks are solved. Below we look at how rewards are derived, and we learn that it isn't as straightforward or formulaic as one might think.

Cheating is far easier in pools because the work is usually split up. For the most part, the pools demand the same proof of work that the network requires, but it is often blocks that are of a far lesser difficulty to solve. This means less time and effort, and some ways of cheating by using the work being generated by others or claiming to have done it yourself.

There are also some horrible miners and/or pool operators using Distributed Denial of Service (DDoS) attacks. These are not new in the world of the Internet, and are defined as: *"an attempt to make a machine or network resource unavailable to its intended users…it generally consists of efforts to temporarily or indefinitely interrupt or suspend services of a host connected to the Internet…Perpetrators of DoS attacks typically target sites or services hosted on high-profile web servers such as banks, credit card payment gateways, and even root nameservers."*

They prevent participation by effectively slowing down a server or preventing someone about to solve the block from interacting with the network.

So, it *is* possible to cheat or fraudulently get shares from a pool. To overcome this, many pools have created unique approaches. Let's look at them one by one:

- Slush - BPM is Bitcoin Pooled Mining and it uses the "slush" approach that features a scoring system that is designed to reduce the desire to switch between pools during a round of calculation. It gives recent "shares" a more substantial weight than earlier ones and is effectively making it more lucrative to remain active in the current pool rather than shopping around for solutions.

- Metahash - puddinpop is another pool that has created a unique way to work around potential cheating. Its participants have to generate hashes and metahashes. The latter are hashes of a very large section of generated hashes. The puddinpop server checks that the metahashes are correct as a proof of work protocol.

Essentially, this prevents any participant from holding on to good blocks (preventing others from benefiting from the calculations). Rewards are based on the number of the metahashes submitted. Additionally, blocks have many keys in the transaction, and this gives the miner rewards in proportion to their contribution to the total block.

- PPS - This is a pay-per-share method that was first used by the pool BitPenny. It gives a payout for each share solved. The pool will have an existing balance, and the miner is able to take their reward immediately without hanging around waiting for the entire block to be found. This tends to be one of the easiest forms of mining because variance is limited, but the pool operator does have to assume a lot of risk. To overcome this, the PPS approach tends to payout a lot lower than other pools.

- Eligius - This is a sort of combination of the slush and the metahash approaches. The miners have to submit their proof of work in order to get shares, and then they get paid immediately. However, when block rewards are distributed they are divided equally between all of the "shares" since the last block solution. Any remaining rewards from "stale" or unsolved blocks are put into the next block and a miner must earn at least 0.67108864 in Bitcoins to be paid.

- Triplemining - This uses a pool of medium size and follows a sort of pyramid structure. Your share grows substantially because redistributes 1% of each block found. The way it works is relatively complex, but is summarized like this: You have a "minipool" that includes yourself and a few friends involved in mining. You have a few shares found in a block, and because of this the pool gets 1% of the value for each share. If the hash rate of the minipool is bigger than or equal to your own, the part you take is far bigger than if you were independent.

- P2P Pool - This is similar to Eligius and puddinpop in that it pays out for generation of a block. It divides the reward between the most recent shares in the block chain.

How do you know which to use? We cannot answer that one for you. We can give you a list of the most current and popular choices, and their size in relation to most of the pools:

Name of Guild or	Date	Number of Blocks Found

Pool	Started	between Jan and Nov 2013
50BTC	11/11/2011	6973
ABCPool.co	8/2/2011	n/a
alvarez.sfek.kz	4/19/2012	n/a
ASICMiner	n/a	1950
BitClockers	5/27/2011	16
BitCoinMining.co	8/13/2013	n/a
BitcoinPool.com	3/8/2011	9

BitMinter	6/26/2011	2758
Bitparking	1/8/2012	48
BTC Guild	5/9/2011	15661
BTC Oxygen	11/1/2012	n/a
BTCDig	7/4/2013	n/a
BTCMine	3/11/2011	60
BTCmow	5/31/2013	n/a
btcmp.com	6/28/2011	n/a

BTCPoolman	3/1/2013	n/a
BTCWarp	7/29/2011	n/a
Coinotron	7/6/2011	12
DeepBit	2/26/2011	1252
Eclipse Mining Consortium	6/14/2011	2147
Eligius	4/27/2011	896
GHash.IO	7/1/2013	n/a
Give Me COINS	8/12/2013	n/a

Horrible Horrendous TT	8/29/2012	595
MaxBTC	3/15/2012	66
mining.bitcoin.cz	11/27/2010	5095
Multipool	3/15/2012	n/a
Ozcoin	6/7/2011	1754
P2Pool	6/17/2011	514
PolMine	6/13/2011	259
pool.itzod.ru	8/1/2011	666

Triplemining	6/28/2011	95

Take the time to research the various pools, their hash rates, the approaches they use, and their success rate or "luck" in order to make the right choices. This may not be the route for you, or even of interest to you, but it is well worth exploring.

Moving Forward

In the next chapter we are going to consider the idea of using Bitcoins as well as investing in them. Hopefully you now have a thorough understanding of the foundation on which Bitcoins exist.

They are virtual, rely on open source software created only a few years ago, and until they really took off were considered mostly hypothetical. They exist because people believe in this method of currency.

Before you scoff at that idea, just remember that over time some other improbable materials had value that allowed them to be used as money, including pepper corns, sea shells, and tulip bulbs.

Additionally, the U.S. economy is a "fiat" system too. Fiat translates loosely to "faith" and that means that the value of the U.S. dollar is what it is because that is what the market believes it should be valued at.

So, this allows us to now see that Bitcoins are not so farfetched or outlandish as early naysayers indicated. To further understand their value, let's move to the next chapter and ask ourselves if we should be using them.

Chapter Three

Should You Use Bitcoins?

Bitcoins were created as a currency with a value that could not be diluted by a central authority (think of America's Federal Reserve and how it can manipulate the value of the dollar).

As the owner of Bitcoins you can use them with total anonymity (which is why they have the unfortunate association with organized and online crime). This anonymity is appealing to many because it means that websites, banks, and any other organizations will be entirely unable to track or collect data on purchases.

Today, the Bitcoin system is actively creating new Bitcoins every single day, but it is also designed to come to a complete end when there are 21 million Bitcoins in circulation. This is anticipated as occurring around 2140.

Deflation and Inflation

When this time arrives, the value of any Bitcoin is going to naturally increase. This is because it is known as a "deflationary currency", and for some it is a big problem.

Why? Essentially the system has a finite number of Bitcoins available. When demand rises, the value of the Bitcoins increase and this is going to force the prices for goods or services to decline.

This is deflation - and this could lead to the failure of Bitcoins as an effective currency because people will begin to hoard them rather than actually use them. The good news is that most experts do not anticipate this happening at any time soon.

Until then, the simple fact that Bitcoin is actually controlled by the masses tends to indicate that it is going to flourish. Think of examples such as Linux and it is easy to see that if open source software and the public good come together - it is going to evolve and survive.

Let's take a moment to compare deflation to inflation in order to understand the benefits of Bitcoins. We already looked at the fiat currencies at work in many parts of the world and we know what this sort of system means. Money is given value not because of its physical characteristics, i.e. it is made of silver or gold, but because a regulatory agency says it is worth a set amount and consumers agree to that amount.

When explained this way, our current monetary system sounds insane and fraught with peril. The treasury or government (as well as a number of outside forces and influences) can effectively set the value on currency. This is what gives rise to inflation as well as a long list of financial dilemmas and disasters. Let's just look at inflation...

Inflation 101

Governments can print as much money as they like, and groups like the Federal Reserve can help to create ongoing problems by allowing the printing to occur. This is often used to help a government meet its national debts, but it doesn't actually grow that economy.

Here's a simple illustration:

You have one million dollar bills in circulation. As a government you decide to double the number of dollar bills in circulation. That now cuts the value of each dollar in half. The vendor selling a product for one dollar now has to demand two dollars to make it worth the same as it was before the new money appeared.

That is inflation, and it forces the prices for goods and services to increase while simultaneously decreasing the purchase power of buyers. Bitcoins have been designed to eliminate this risk because it is currency that is decentralized -

it is in *your* hands and control. However, as you have already learned, that is not its only benefit.

The Benefits of Bitcoin

Even with all that you now know about them you still may find yourself asking: Why should the general public take so readily to something like Bitcoin?

After all, it is a relatively untested thing that could lead to the loss of investment should the currency collapse.

Forget Inflation

The first thing to remember is that Bitcoin was fundamentally designed to avoid inflation by having that maximum number available (21 million). Unlike dollars, there cannot be any artificial increase in available Bitcoins created by some regulatory agency. The algorithm was designed to create that set amount and then the calculations run out. Miners will be unable to generate any further coins as they will have processed all of the possible hashes.

Forget Manipulation

Bitcoin was also meant to remove a lot of the financial controls of centralized banking and investment firms. Remember, we are living in the post-2008 era in which global banking and investment firms proved that they could not be trusted to guard market stability. Although today, many of the firms that weathered the financial storms (and which some of them helped to cause) have recovered and are showing huge profits, the markets have not stabilized.

This makes the average investor or consumer wonder just how to protect themselves and even thwart the profit margins of the major economic firms. One of the simplest ways to do that is to effectively cut off the money these groups make from every transaction, account, etc.

Bitcoins allows this through the simplicity of the system. In fact, you hold your money - not a bank - and you can often conduct transactions for small or even no fees.

The Power in Your Hands with Bitcoins

Just consider the things you might do each day to use your Bitcoins instead of supporting global banking giants, investment firms, and governmental economic systems:

- Rather than using a debit card with its fees and with your assets in the hands of the bank, the acceptance of Bitcoins in real world settings enables you to purchase in total security and privacy while maintaining complete control over personal wealth.

- Entities like PayPal and credit card firms are put at risk for loss of tremendous sums because Bitcoins can work online and in many real world settings - effectively eliminating the need for them;

- Your security is never at risk with Bitcoins the way it is with almost any other form of online shopping. Bitcoin transactions don't ask you to give up private information. Instead, you rely on those two keys: the public key, and the private one;

- Rather than waiting for approval, documentation, and clearance to conduct international financial transactions, two people can use Bitcoins to make the transactions in a few simple and often immediate steps, and in total anonymity; and

- Instead of all currency being valued or devalued by large entities such as a Federal Reserve, the Bitcoin is something that is valued according to supply and demand - a far more accurate method.

This adds up to a sincere need to consider purchasing and using Bitcoins in at least one way. We are going to look at the three most common ways that consumers can start to use Bitcoins effectively.

How to Apply Bitcoins in the Real World

You may hear the arguments for the elimination of the penny from time to time, and this tends to cause a tremendous furor. However, ask yourself how often you use them. Then, ask yourself just how often you carry cash any longer.

Most people are carrying less cash and relying less and less on paper money and coins. The world has gone plastic, mobile, or virtual. This tells us that Bitcoins are a sort of "no brainer" or obvious next step…just not yet.

They are already being put to use and accepted widely, but right now they are less than five years old and still not a solid part of the consumer psyche. Until they are, it can seem difficult to find a use for them. Fortunately, they are an entity that goes "hand in hand" with the online world, and so you may be surprised at how easy it can be to begin using them, buying them, trading them, and storing them.

Payment System

For the most part, you will read that Bitcoin is something seen as a tool for those who want to make online payments privately and without restriction.

Unlike sites such as PayPal or typical credit card networks that let you pay or accept money, the Bitcoin network is far more comprehensive. You can spend, trade, and move your money around as easily and cheaply as you would send an email over the Internet. It is not limited purely to commercial transactions, but is an entire financial system.

Additionally, you do all of this without any revelations as to your identity. This is how some groups have abused the system (headlines talk about drug deals and organized crime) and used Bitcoins to fund money laundering and worse, it does demonstrate that Bitcoins are a reliable way to pay for something online too.

To date, many major vendors have started to accept Bitcoins for purchases. We already pointed out that Richard Branson is allowing passengers hoping to travel to outer space to pay for their enormous fares using Bitcoins, but many vendors are now accepting them as well.

The key to using them in this way is to have established a "wallet" into which all Bitcoins are placed for storage. To learn about that, we'll look at the next way of using Bitcoins - as a form of currency.

Currency

Let's say that you want to travel.

- You would need to make sure your credit card or bank card would work within your destination.

- You might take cash and have it changed into the local currency.

- You may even need to get traveler's checks that ensure you have access to cash when you arrive.

- You would also need to be able to gain access to any online banking systems required to access or move money while abroad.

Imagine how much better it would be if all you needed was Bitcoin software on your mobile device.

With it you would be able to do everything needed - pay, get local currency, and relocate funds if needed - but without any threats associated with hackers, high fees from financial institutions, and with complete anonymity.

It would all start with your Bitcoin wallet…

The Bitcoin Wallet

There is more than one way to look at the Bitcoin wallet, however, they all tend to provide the same function:

They will store the Private Keys you need to access your complete Digital Signature and spend or use your "funds".

After that, they are capable of sending money to others in the Bitcoin network, or accepting Bitcoins from them. The wallet can also be used through a mobile device to send payments to vendors accepting Bitcoins too.

However, people rarely "store" Bitcoins in a physical wallet because there is no actual, minted or printed currency (though some enthusiasts are making tokens with the security keys contained in them).

Remember that it comes down to the Private and Public keys and the Digital Signature that is a sort of validation process and this begins with a computer screen indicating that series of numbers and letters. Thus, some people write them down as a way of storing them, some use computers and devices, and some websites.

The Most Common Wallets

Essentially, there are three ways to have a wallet:

- Desktop or laptop - Earlier in the book we said that anyone hoping to mine for Bitcoins would need to download the Bitcoin client. As soon as you do that, you have actually created a wallet.

  How? The client may be a method for relaying transactions across the network, but it also enables the owner to create their address (Public Key) for sending and for receiving Bitcoins. The client also stores the Private Key too.

  This means you can use the **Bitcoin-Qt client**, http://bitcoin.org/en/download, or you can explore some of the emerging wallet programs that include **Multibit**, https://multibit.org/, **Hive**, http://www.grabhive.com/, **Armory**, https://bitcoinarmory.com/, and **DarkWallet**, https://darkwallet.unsystem.net/, among others.

- Mobile - An "app" that works on a Smartphone, mobile wallets will keep the Private Key for any of your Bitcoin addresses, and will also let you pay for things when merchants accept Bitcoin payments.

This can be done with barcode scanning, with NFC options (such as tapping the phone to a reader and paying without any further data input), or with a direct transfer across the peer to peer network. (This is also how many people do real world Bitcoin exchanges).

The most commonly used mobile wallets include the Android friendly **Bitcoin Wallet**, **Blockchain**, **Mycelium Bitcoin Wallet**, **Kipochi**, **Coinbase**.

- Online - While storing the Bitcoin keys on a laptop or desktop may feel safe, there is always a threat of hacking. This is why a lot of people turn to web-based wallets. These store the Private Keys in an online vault, and yet some of them allow linking to your mobile device or to a wallet synced to the desktop as well.

Why use online? Not only is it a safer way of maintaining the Bitcoin wallet's safety, it gives you access from anywhere, and guarantees against loss should anything happen to the computer. There are many horror stories of Bitcoin owners wiping a hard drive or suffering computer loss and seeing all of their Bitcoins going with it.

Additionally, the best online wallet providers are also creating a double layer of protection. For example, **Strongcoin** https://www.strongcoin.com/ is a preferred provider of online wallet services and it encrypts your Private Keys before they are sent to the server. This means that it is only the account holder who can ever see, know, or access the data. Even if hackers succeeded in gaining access, the data would prove meaningless.

Other names in online wallets include **Coinbase**, https://coinbase.com/, and **Blockchain**, https://blockchain.info/.

- Optional - Some people use paper, meaning they write things down and keep everything offline and free of threat from hackers. However, we'd advocate for one of the three methods above instead of this labor intensive and less than certain approach. Also, storing everything to something like a thumb drive or freestanding hard drive is not advisable as these too can be damaged or lost.

To begin using Bitcoins for payment or as currency and investment means having that wallet.

Using Bitcoin as Currency

Once you have the wallet you can begin using it to pay for goods and services in a diversity of ways and locations. Such as? Well, the most up to date list has to include the following categories:

- Regular, everyday purchases of goods and services online - The trend in Bitcoins is just starting to "catch on", but it won't be long until most sites are finding ways to accept payments from Bitcoin wallets. Right now it is best to use aggregators and directories that list the sites glad to take your Bitcoins.

Some of the most reliable are:

- o **Coinmap**

  http://coinmap.org/

- o **SpendBitcoins.com**

  https://www.spendbitcoins.com/places/

- o **UseBitcoins**

  http://usebitcoins.info/

- o **Bitcoin Marketplace**

  http://bitcoinmarketplace.net/

- o **Cryptothrift**

  https://cryptothrift.com/

- o **Bitmarket**

  http://www.reddit.com/r/bitmarket

- o **Flibbr**

  http://flibbr.com/

You may also already know that some major online service providers readily accept Bitcoin payments. For example, the major blogging engine known as WordPress has been accepting Bitcoin payments for a while.

Other online services and hosting companies accepting credits include Spotify, AirVPN, Playstation, and more. The credits are available from the **BitCoinCodes,** http://bitcoincodes.com/, website. Sites such as **NameCheap.com** also just accepts direct Bitcoin payments for domain registry services.

It is not all that surprising that web based services should be willing to accept Bitcoin payment. It allows them a tremendously affordable method of obtaining payment, it keeps transactions secure and private, and it lets them work with anyone in the world.

Sites like PayPal and most credit card companies can block out a lot of payments due to governmental or in-house policies, and Bitcoin eliminates such controls.

As an example, countries with trade embargos are now open to the global markets if vendors and producers in those countries find ways to accept and send Bitcoins. An online shoe seller known as "Persian Shoes" does just that and allows shoe makers in Iran to do trade outside of their embargoed borders.

- There are also Bitcoin specific shops set up in many parts of the world. However, do check to see shipping policies as some are U.S. only, Europe only, etc. The following are recommended:

- **BitcoinShop.us** - Whether it is toys or health and beauty products, this site specializes in Bitcoin purchases.

- **BitcoinStore.com** - Specializing in electronics it is Bitcoin-only and U.S. based.

- **MemoryDealers.com** - Emphasizes the gear needed to mine Bitcoin.

- Using Bitcoins in real world establishments - In an interesting article in *Wired*, a group of Bitcoin enthusiasts is described as having weekly meetings in a Tokyo café. There the group discusses Bitcoins and pays for their food and drink with them. This identifies a distinct trend in the Bitcoin movement, and that is the rapid expansion of bars and restaurants happy to accept Bitcoin payment.

Not only is it becoming more and more common for small businesses of this kind to take Bitcoin payments, but there is also a major spike in online ordering and takeout service using Bitcoin payment systems too.

The website **Foodler.com** allows visitors to browse a list of 13k restaurants around the globe and then use special Bitcoin credits to make purchases at the restaurants on the site. So, ask your favorite coffee house or restaurant if they are onboard the Bitcoin trend.

There is also Bitcoin.Travel which is a website meant to facilitate the difficulties in arranging travel without the use of traditional credit cards. The site also emphasizes vendors already taking Bitcoin payments.

- Online casinos - This is something that really helped to grow the Bitcoin trend as it has been historically difficult for online gamers to fund their accounts. Now, the privacy of Bitcoin allows gamers from all over the world to play almost anywhere they would like.

- Buying gift cards - If you are finding that spending Bitcoin is more challenging than you anticipated, it is possible to convert them into real world currency by the purchase of gift cards.

  This is such a common requirement that a list of sites is now converting digital currency into useable cards at some of the world's leading retail establishments. For example, you can shop at "big box" stores like Walmart, or head online to buy directly from Nike using cards acquired with Bitcoins. The gift card vendors happy to accept Bitcoins includes:

  - **iTradeBTC**
    http://www.itradebtc.com/

- **GiftCardZen**

  https://www.giftcardzen.com/

- **Gyft**

  http://www.gyft.com/bitcoin

- **eGifter**

  http://www.egifter.com/bitcoin

- **GiftCardBTC**

  https://giftcardbtc.com/

- Donations - Finally, it should be noted that the Libertarian political party in the United States was the first to accept donations in the form of Bitcoin. Since then a lot of social action and global campaigns have recognized the benefits of Bitcoin and the Bitcoin wiki page has an enormous list of the organizations, or projects currently capable of taking your Bitcoin donations https://en.bitcoin.it/wiki/Donation-accepting_organizations_and_projects.

What you may also wonder about is using Bitcoin as part of an investment portfolio. After all, it is something that has shown tremendous, almost frightening, growth and that makes it an appealing investment option.

Investing

Naturally, meteoric growth is not always the right reason to invest in something. In fact, many point out that such rapid increases in value are more indicative of a bubble rather than a long term investment option. Of course, it could also be argued that anything the Winkelvoss twins invest heavily in is something to give a lot of attention to as well.

However, there is more to be considered here. For example, a computer algorithm created the concept of Bitcoins. Rather than a human mind and all of the variants that could influence the outcome of a system. Bitcoin is not vulnerable to monetary policies dictated by individuals with varying agendas. It is a cryptocurrency, decentralized, and a system that is not open to fraud.

Investing in them, however, has to be done according to the same rules or guidelines as all other types of investments - with your needs and budget in mind.

For example, speak to anyone about gold investments in the past few years and even the most liberal would say that committing more than 20% of the available capital to precious metals (even in the face of their epic growth) is unwise at the very least.

So, if you want to begin investing in Bitcoin, take that advice along with the typical "buy low" advice too. For example, in late November 2013 the daily pricing of Bitcoins increased higher and higher reaching over $1000 before the end of the month. Only a few months before it had not yet broken the $400 mark.

Savvy buyers would want to use the history of Bitcoin pricing as a gauge and wait for the anticipated decline in pricing.

As one expert suggested in Digital Trends, "*Wait a little while and you could buy a Bitcoin for a fraction of what it is today - and then wait till the price jumps back up, cash out, and go buy an apartment.*"

While that is a bit of an exaggeration, there is some truth in it. Yes, the pricing is that volatile now, but as we have repeatedly indicated, it is a deflationary currency and will cap at 21 million Bitcoins at some point in the future. This is a healthy way to develop currency, but there will be those who hoard the Bitcoins in a hope of cashing out to a substantial sum.

Whether this is good or bad for the development of Bitcoins is to be seen. However, what it all adds up to for those interested in Bitcoins is that they are a remarkably savvy form of investment for short or long term holdings.

Obtaining Bitcoins for Investment

How do you get them for investment? You use some of the methods already described, plus the following:

- Use a Bitcoin exchange - These are places where you can exchange Bitcoins for other currencies or vice versa. They can have connections to "real world" banks and financial agencies so some transactions are not invisible. However, it does make it easy to move your converted Bitcoins into bank accounts if cashing out your holdings;

- Live exchanges - This may seem like something out of a spy thriller, but it is also something happening on a weekly basis in high schools, coffee shops, and more. Essentially, you may arrange to meet with someone to exchange currency for Bitcoins. The Bitcoins are usually transferred via a mobile application once the currency has been given to the Bitcoin owner. This is a good way to obtain Bitcoins without any purchase fees, etc. They do vary, but the Bitcoin wiki lists the top exchanges known for safety and reliability https://en.bitcoin.it/wiki/Buying_bitcoins; and

- Buying physical Bitcoins - Though they are not actual forms of physical currency, it is possible to obtain minted coins. For example, one engineer in Utah is actually minting Bitcoin tokens that have their cryptographic codes protected by tamper-proof holographic seals. This would protect the data you need to use them and also ensure that no hacker could ever "steal" the information. Some people also just log their keys in paper journals or "offline" computers and run spreadsheets assessing how much their investments are yielding.

As already indicated, it is entirely up to you as an investor to guarantee that you are making the wisest financial decisions.

Though it may seem like the ideal time to get in on the Bitcoin market, remember it is volatile and evolving. There are bound to be ups and downs, and the smartest buyers are those who wait for dips in pricing in order to maximize returns.

Also remember that it Bitcoins do have some issues evolving around them in terms of taxes, legality, and limitations due to their abuse by some dubious groups and individuals.

In order to understand how this may impact your decision to invest or begin using Bitcoins, let's look at our final subject - you and your Bitcoins.

Chapter Four

You and Your Bitcoins

By this time it is probably quite obvious to you that Bitcoins are an inevitability. Though there are around 80 different cryptocurrencies and/or virtual currencies, it is only Bitcoin that has really caught on.

Why? It has to do with many different facets of it, and these include:

- The algorithm ensures that this is not an inflationary currency;

- Many online vendors and organizations have already stepped up to support its growth through acceptance of Bitcoins or through the creation of applications and gear to make them easier to obtain;

- Many real world vendors are encouraging their use for goods and services;

- They are a natural extension of our debit and credit card, as well as our online and mobile fixation (after all, some of us go weeks without touching actual money);

- It is decentralized, peer to peer, and open source that operates along the same lines as a fiat currency but without the interference of governments and/or financial institutions;

- It can be directly exchanged for currency;

- It is a computer designed system not open to human fallibility and greed; and

- It "democratizes" the world of finance by erasing national borders and boundaries.

Obviously, it has a lot to say for itself and this is precisely why it is flourishing. Of course, for all of the "pros" there are going to be some "cons" too. Let's look at them.

The Inevitable Cons

- Legality - What the experts, thus far, have said about the legality of Bitcoins varies. They are, naturally, of extreme interest to all law enforcement and tax authorities. After all, Bitcoin can result in a tremendous impact on the financial systems in place.

  For instance, where can it fit into the existing structures where taxes and income are concerned? What about the general market? What does this mean for the IRS and other revenue sources for the government?

  It is too early in the evolution of Bitcoin to know just how governments are going to seek to handle it. What many say is that it really depends on "who" you are and how you intend to use it. As an example, Mt. Gox (the world's largest exchange) has been under the scrutiny of the U.S. government a few times. The reasons cited include money laundering, Homeland Security issues, and more.

There are also those who view the anonymity of Bitcoin is a definite "pro" for many. Unfortunately, that includes the "bad guys" of the world too. After all, there is zero "paper trail" behind the use of it. No one will know if or what you have used the transactions for.

So, it makes it easy for the criminally minded to conduct all kinds of activities - from selling drugs to auctioning antiquities on illegal or underground sites.

However, it also makes the average consumer happy because they don't have vendors tagging their transactions left and right.

For example, a website such as Amazon.com will definitely track purchases and keep tabs on everything that you do. With the use of Bitcoin wallets you can essentially operate without giving over any details or financial data. Everything that you purchase can remain a secret.

What does this mean to the consumer hoping to use it? Very little. For now, it is best to keep a watchful eye on what government regulators want to do with Bitcoin. Currently, they are going after exchanges, and not the individual users.

- Taxes - To keep it as simple as possible - any gains you have in your Bitcoin investments is to be reported as capital gains. However, who is to know when you've profited? No one.

Thus, someone making a small fortune on their Bitcoin investment may be accidentally (we will assume it is!) committing tax fraud simply by failing to report their earnings;

- Hacking - Though the mining system is almost impossible to thwart or to commit fraud upon, there are some risks where security is concerned. This is because there are now groups creating Bitcoin targeted malware and viruses that aim at stealing account details in order to get access to wallets.

  Alternately, they seek to gain control of a computer long enough to harvest the Private Keys and other important data. Because of this, you have to create multiple levels of protection and this tends to ensure against the most prevalent threats.

- Security - One of the most distinct "cons" relating to them is the lack of protection similar to that provided by the bank or credit card company.

For example, the FDIC ensures you get your money if the bank fails. If you lose your Bitcoins in any way - to fraud or to some other reason - they are gone and nothing is going to bring them back.

Fortunately, you are going to be able to easily establish your own protocols for protection that can range from a web based wallet with thorough encryption to offline storage for total safety.

- Not yet widely accepted - Naturally, the one thing that holds back so many from using them is that they are not yet a "commonly accepted" form of currency. This means you can have a bit bank account without the ability to use it in many places. This is bound to change, and is indeed already doing so, but it does indicate a bit of a glitch in the current era.

- Unclear exchanges - Because Bitcoins are not tied to dollars or other currencies, their exchange rates are vague and unclear. The fluctuation in the pricing (which change by the hour when buying and selling is heaviest) makes it even more difficult to ensure the best pricing.

Additionally, there are some commissions and fees that can impact the result of any transaction. This makes many consumers a bit leery of them at the present.

- Deflationary confusion - A lot of people are unclear what deflationary and inflationary currencies mean. This is unfortunate because the deflationary nature of Bitcoins is a major bonus.

For example, they are designed to have a limited supply. The algorithm ensures that coin issuance is going to slow by half every four years. That is why they will not reach their cap of 21 million for a while. This makes them an excellent investment, but they are meant to be used as currency and not hoarded like gold. This is a bit confusing and leads many to worry about the end value.

However, the answer is in plain sight. The value of Bitcoins will be driven up as they start to be used widely and gain broader acceptance around the globe. Thus, using them and investing in them is one of the smartest ways to ensure a good result.

That is really all there is to know about Bitcoins. You now can honestly say that you understand how they are "made" and found. How they are an incredible opportunity for people all over the world, and how they seem to be a natural part of the latest developments in this era of the Internet.

That means it is time to make your plans and introduce Bitcoins to your portfolio or budget.

In Conclusion

The Years Ahead

Based on all that we have reviewed here it is easy to say that Bitcoins are a very savvy investment. They are the wave of the future, and though the algorithm could be changed to accommodate a global demand for more of them, this is not anticipated to be the case.

Instead, they are seen as a way of regulating an economy by creating enough "money" to support fair and democratic trade around the globe. This is why so many experts are saying to go ahead and get yourself a wallet, start buying Bitcoins and even investing small percentages of the portfolio in them.

They also say that watching the markets and keeping tabs on regulators and activities in the Bitcoin world are sound decisions.

Your Bitcoins

How should you get started? Take time to explore the wallet options provided. These are a good way to get a very solid education in how, precisely, Bitcoin buying, trading, and use is being done.

It is a very good idea to choose a wallet that will allow you to easily keep everything encrypted and secure. If you opt to use your desktop or laptop as your wallet, be sure that security is optimized and back up the data to another drive or in a cloud server.

If using a mobile app, realize that it has to sync with a laptop or desktop. Remember too that the Bitcoins are not "sent" to the wallet. The wallet is how you access and use the codes that are yours. The entire Bitcoin history exists in that "ledger", and all of the Bitcoins you would own or use are documented there. The wallet client is what accesses this information.

Your wallet client or program does not have to remain up and running to receive the coins it is owed. Whenever the software is run it updates the entire block and catches up to the current version - ensuring you can use the Bitcoins if desired.

Once you are familiar with the wallet and client, you should start looking at your preferred methods for obtaining Bitcoins. Will you use an exchange? Do live interactions? Join a local club enthusiastic about Bitcoins?

This is the best part about Bitcoin investing and use…learning about this entirely new currency. However, spend the time and really "know your stuff".

Only after you are totally familiar with Bitcoins should you begin using them. Always remember that they have to be broken into bits and pieces if you are going to use them, and that prices have to be "translated" or converted accordingly.

Remember that first pizza ordered online with Bitcoins - it cost 10k coins. That would mean that in today's markets it would cost $10,000! Obviously, in only a few short years things have changed, but you do need to understand just what one Bitcoin is worth in your currency to avoid any costly blunders.

All of this can help your investing too, and if after all that you have learned and experienced you think mining is something of interest for you, you are going to find an enormous array of groups and sites offering advice about the latest hardware, pools, and more.

This could easily become a stream of income if you are willing to do the research and find the optimal investment for your budget and goals.

In the end, Bitcoins are the newest thing on the horizon. They are in their infancy and it does pay to consider if this is a "ground floor" opportunity just waiting for your participation or investment.

Based on the response from some of the world's biggest financial experts (from Richard Branson to the amazing Winklevoss twins) the Bitcoin is the ultimate currency for the new and modern economy. If you want to invest in the future, this is the time to do it and the route to take.

www.ingramcontent.com/pod-product-compliance
Lightning Source LLC
Chambersburg PA
CBHW051726170526
45167CB00002B/823